# Moira Rules

By Selena Millman

# _Moira Rules_
By Selena Millman

ISBN: 978-0-359-74970-6

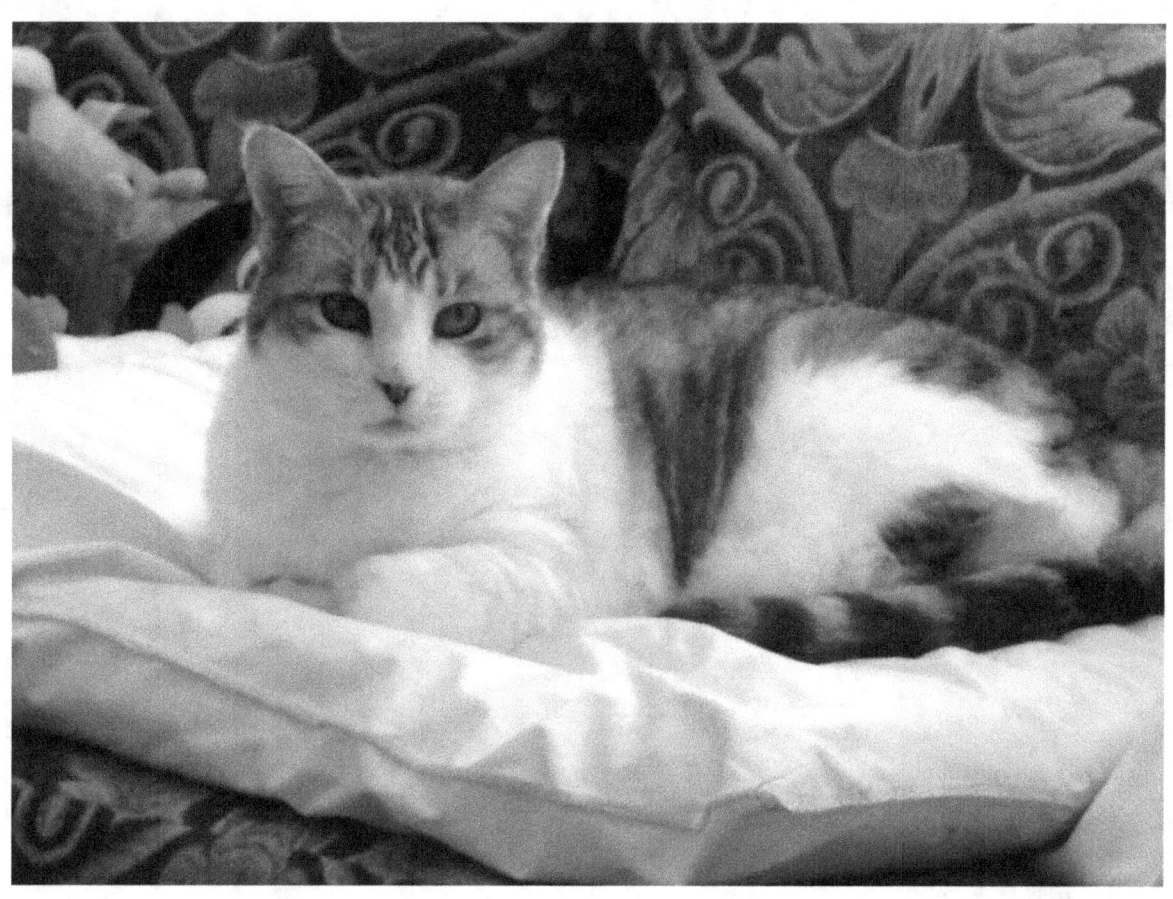

I look like a cat.

Okay, I am a cat.

But I am so much more.

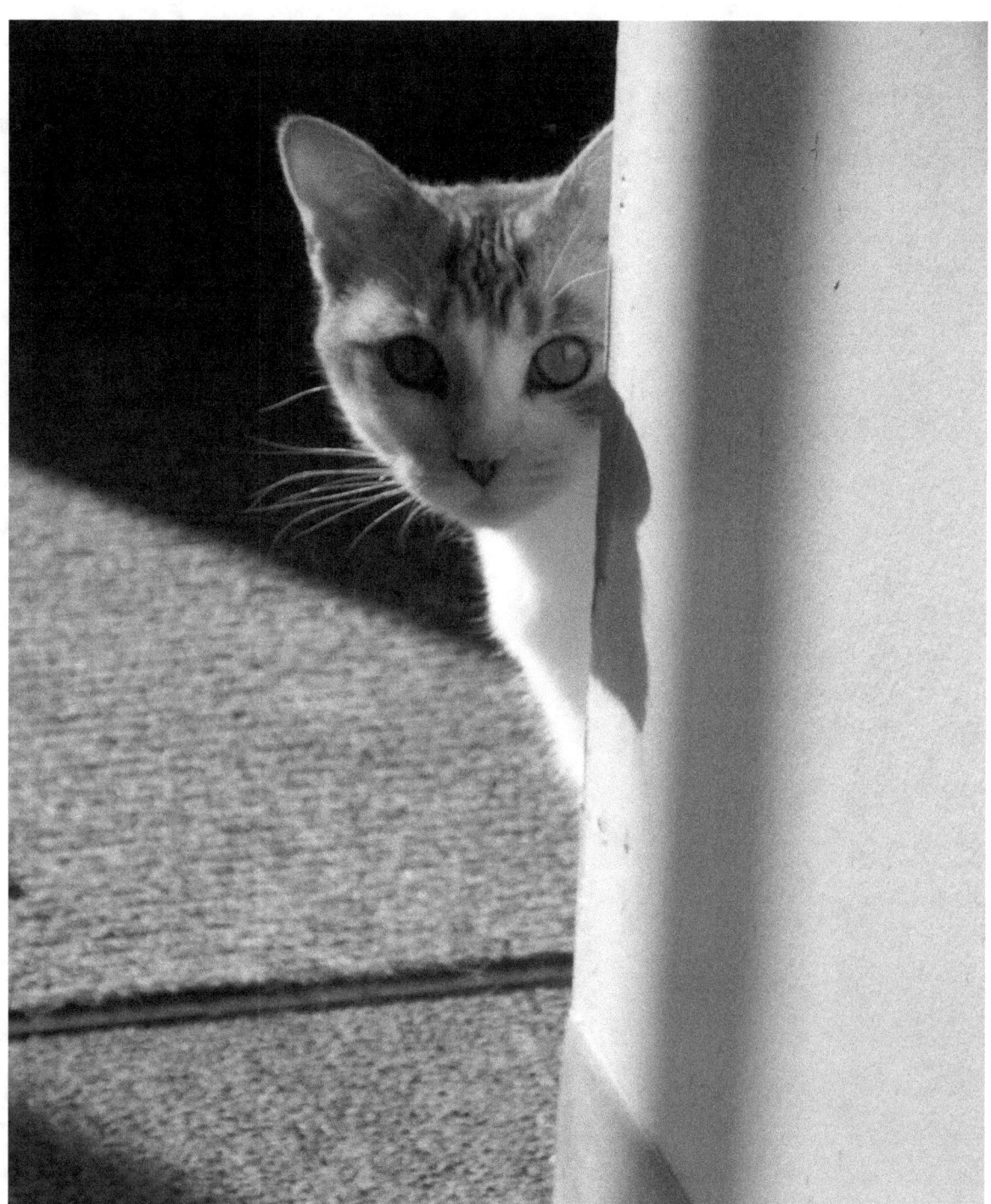

My mommy calls me the Queen.

She's right because I rule the home.

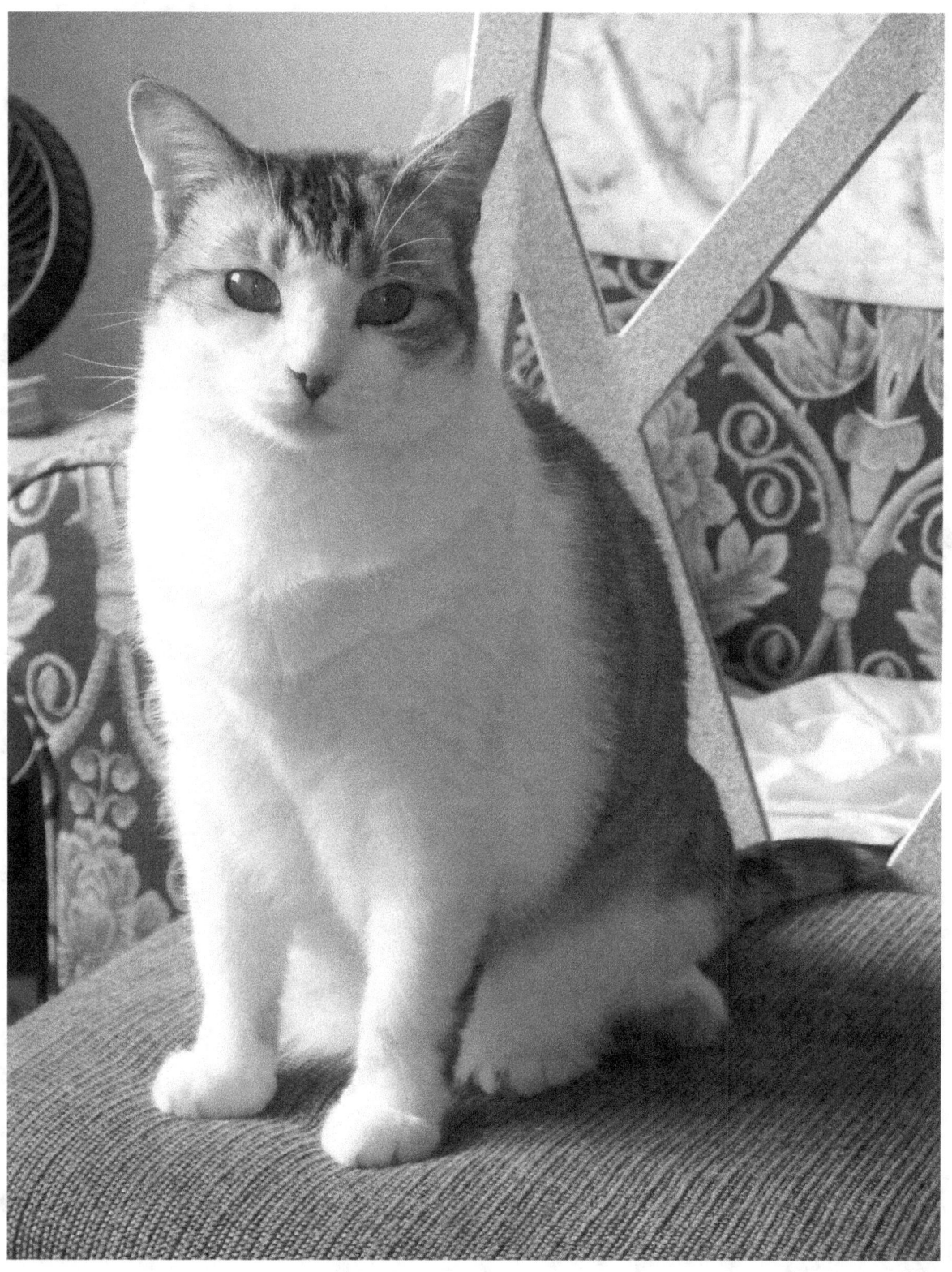

Be good to me and I will love you.

I demand attention.

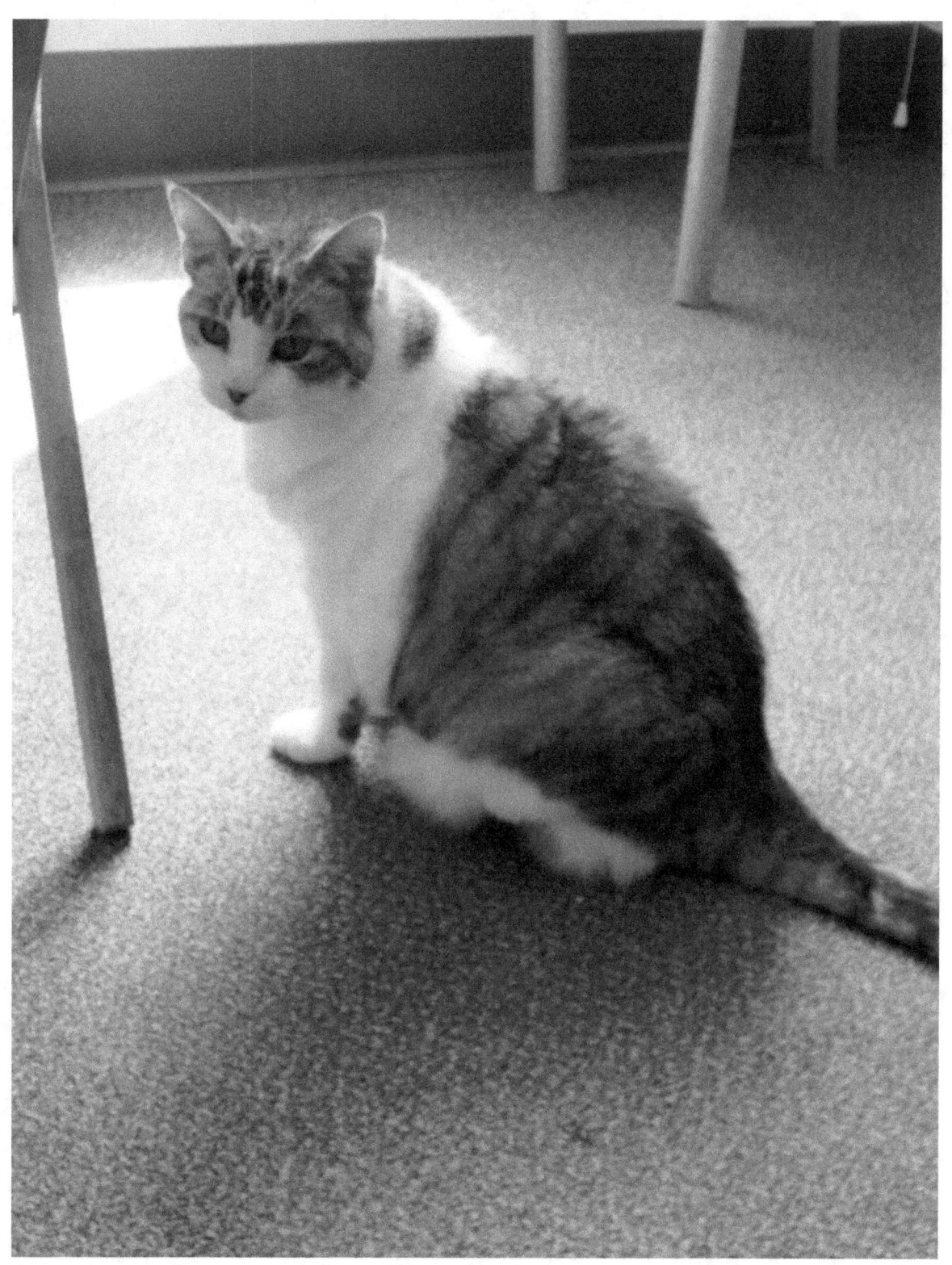

My main goal in life is to spread love.

To my mommy first. Then to others.

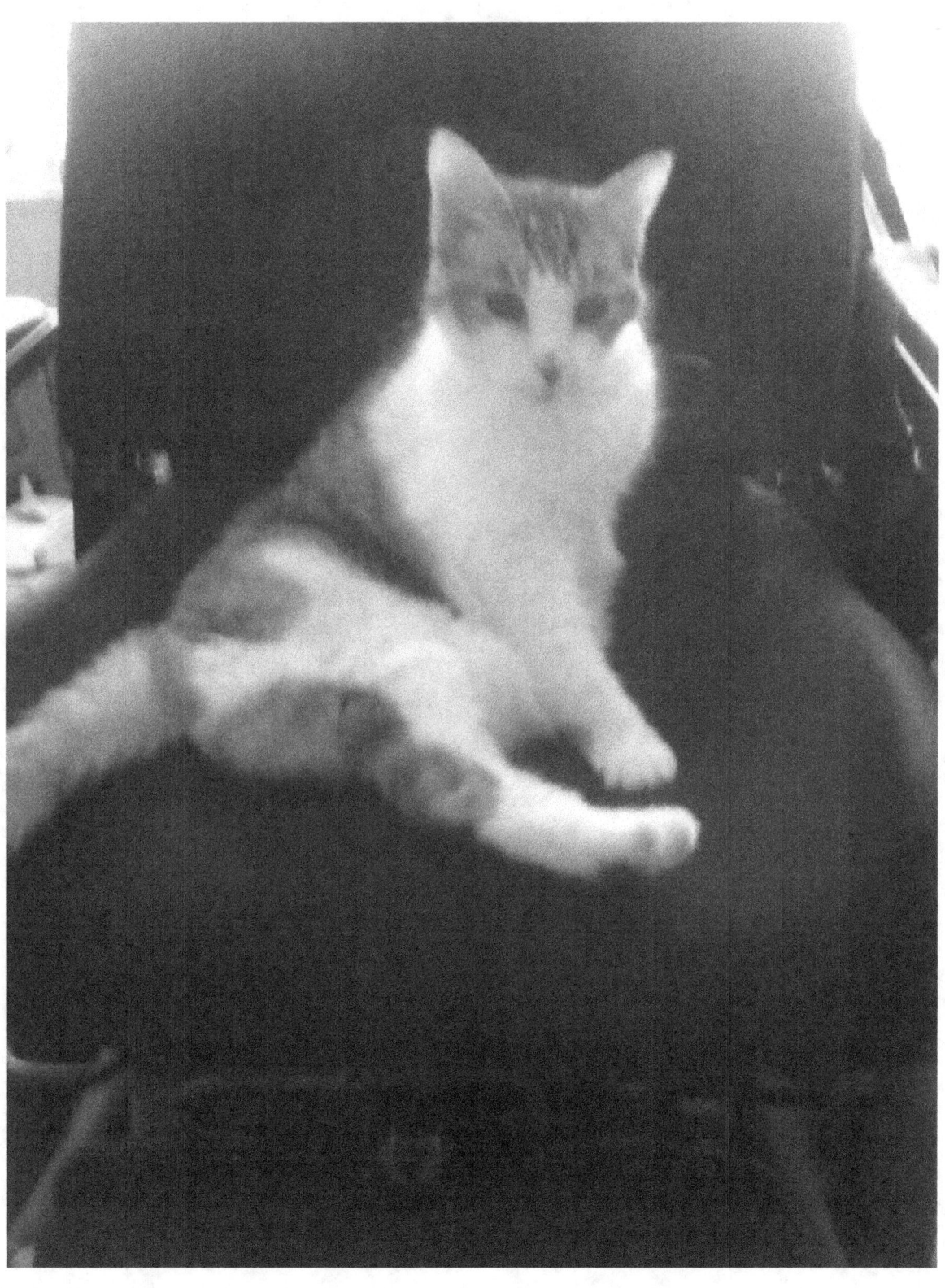

I like to cuddle and snuggle.

Rub me, please.

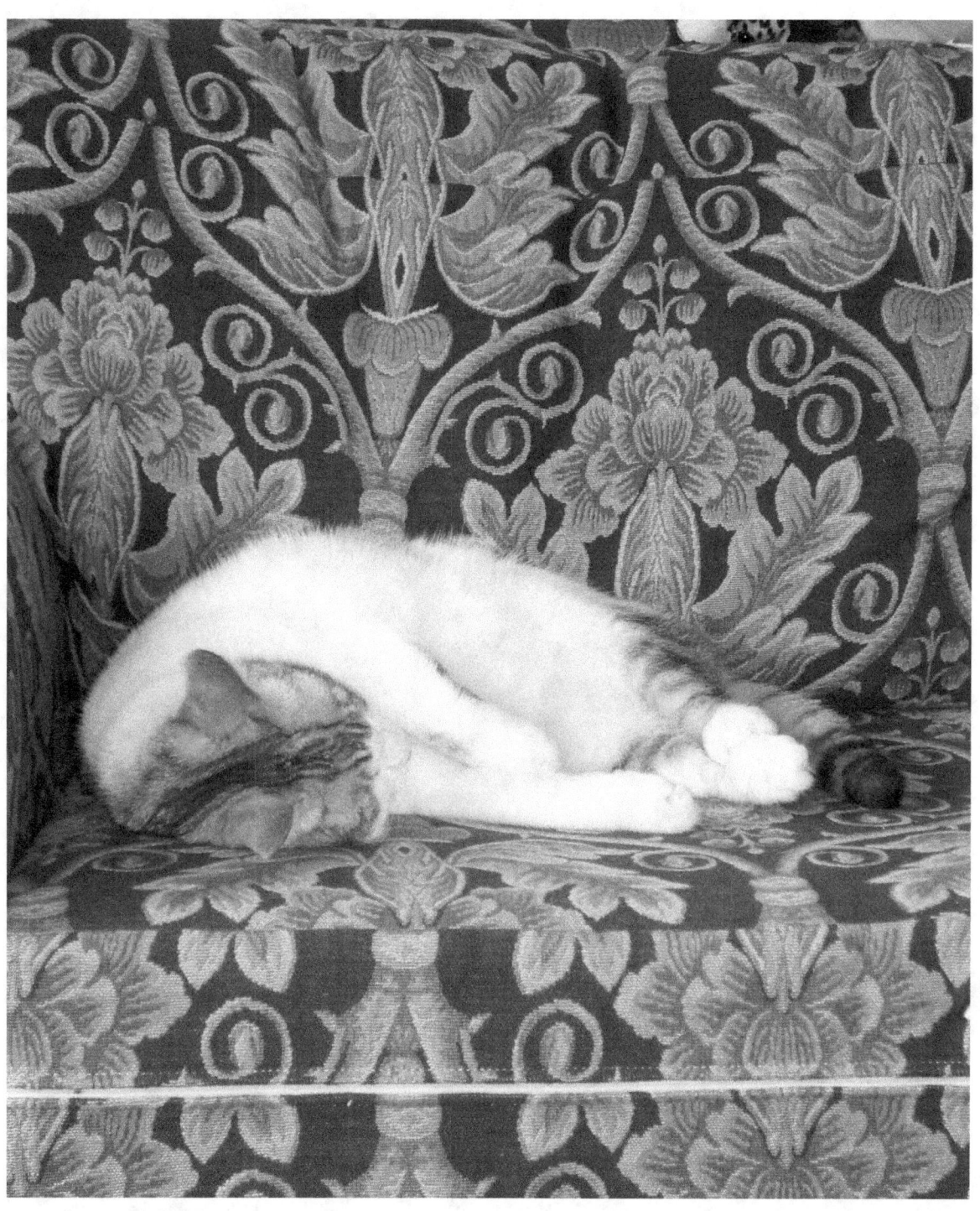

I like to goof around and play.

I do sometimes like to play with things mommy doesn't want
me to play with. Especially pens!

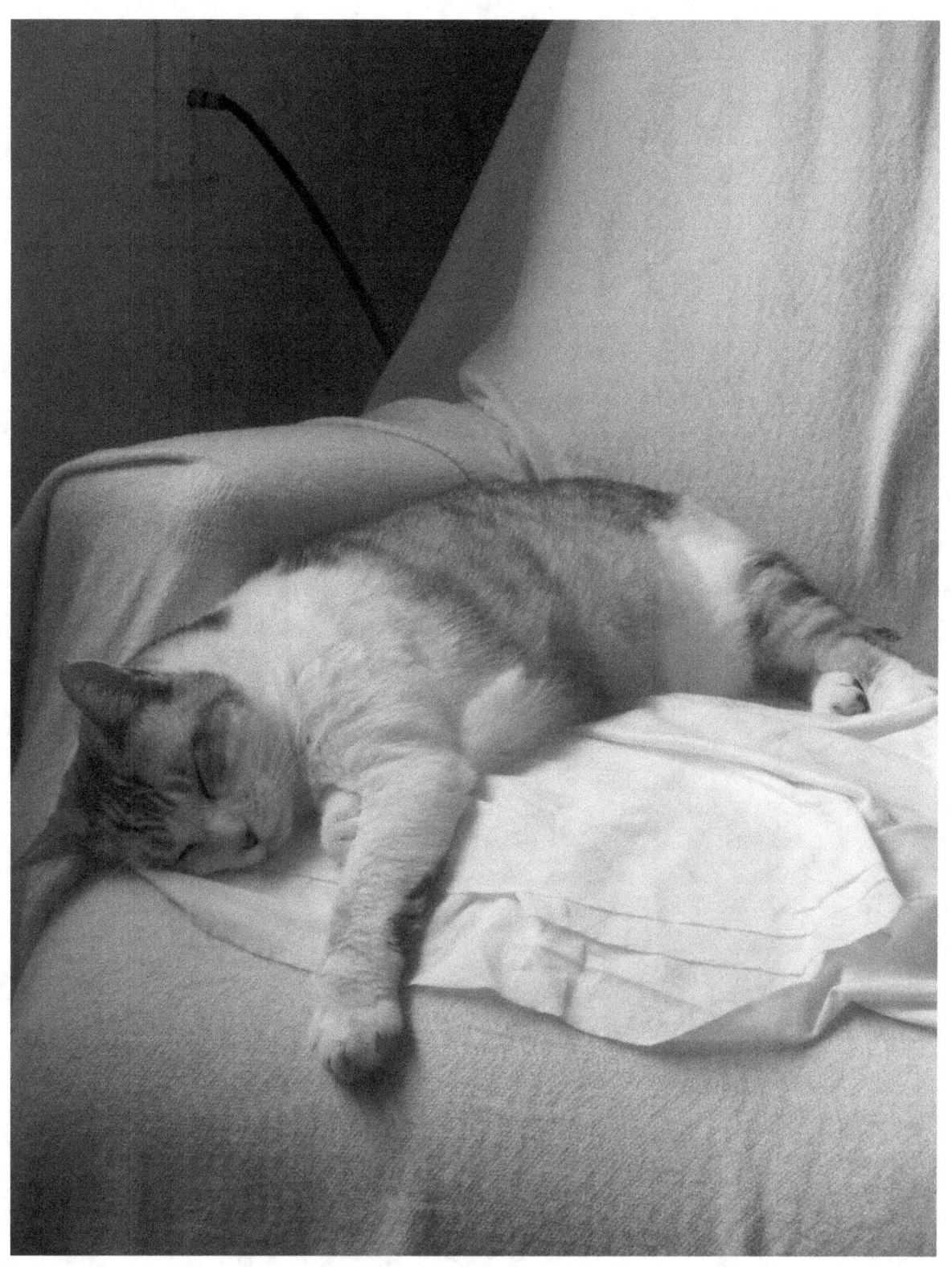

I notice everything.

Don't think I don't see you.

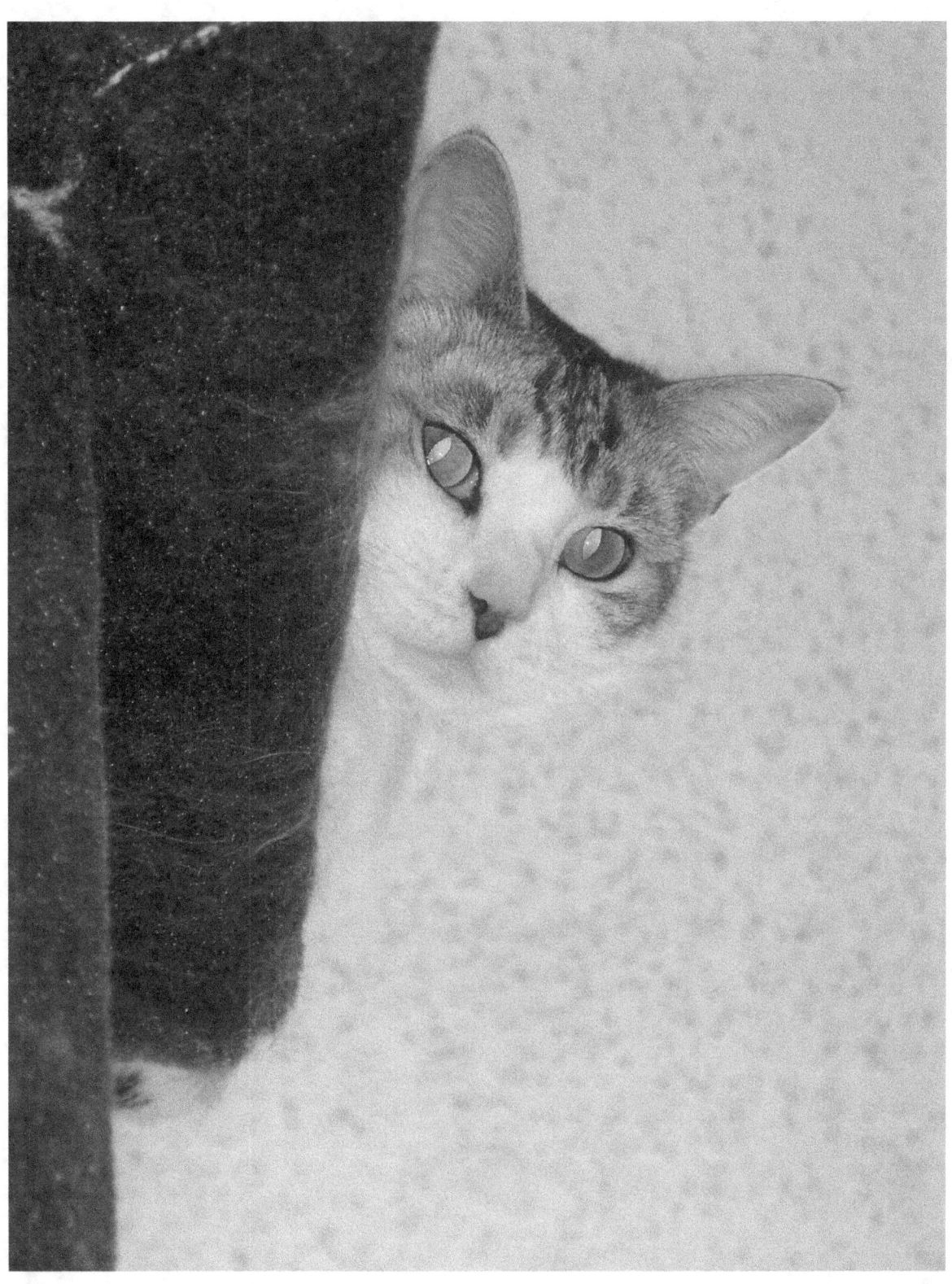

Sometimes I like salmon, shrimp, or chicken.

But I always LOVE tuna. Do you have some?

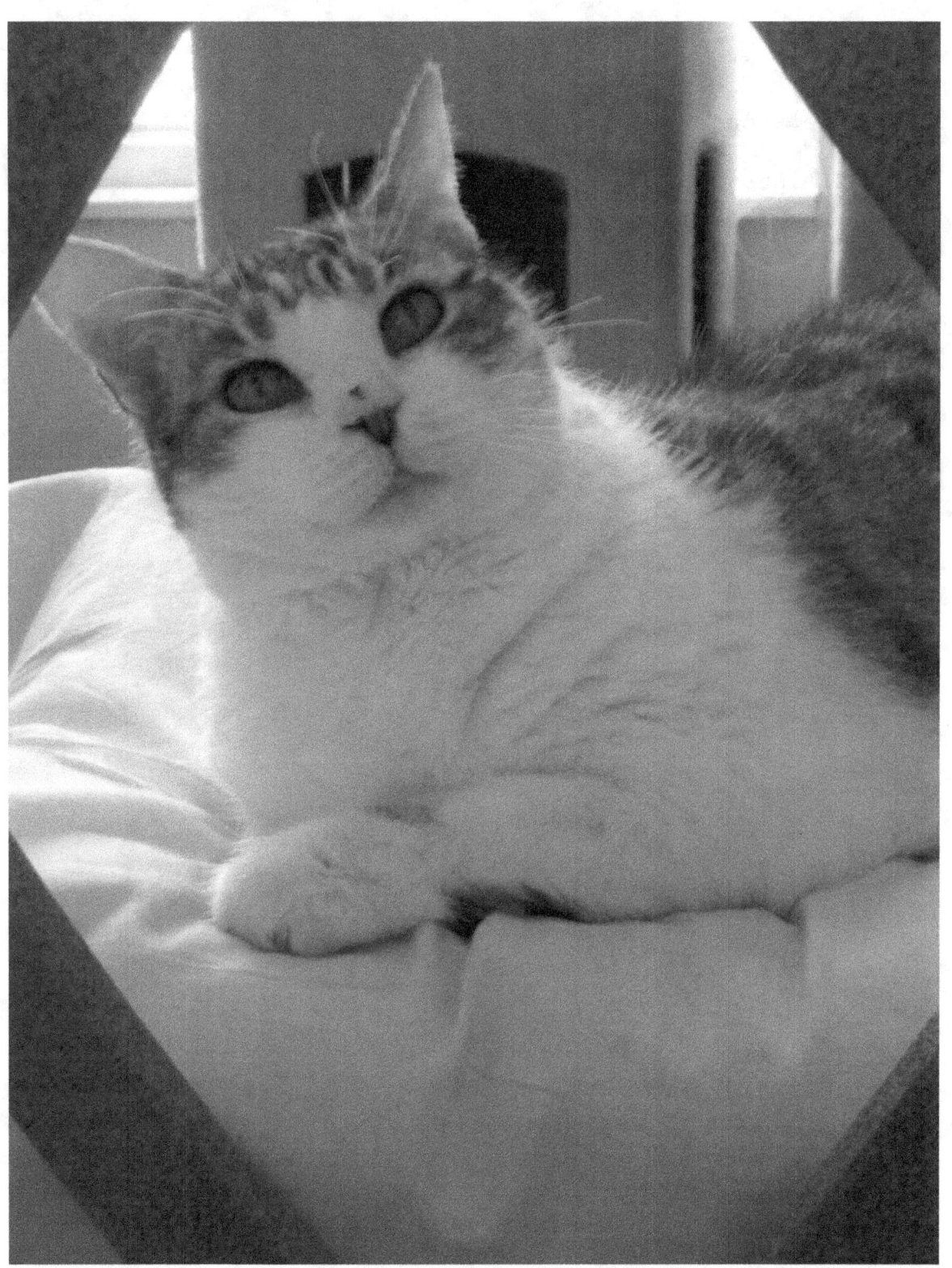

My mommy thinks she adopted me.

Okay, she adopted me.

But I CLAIMED her.

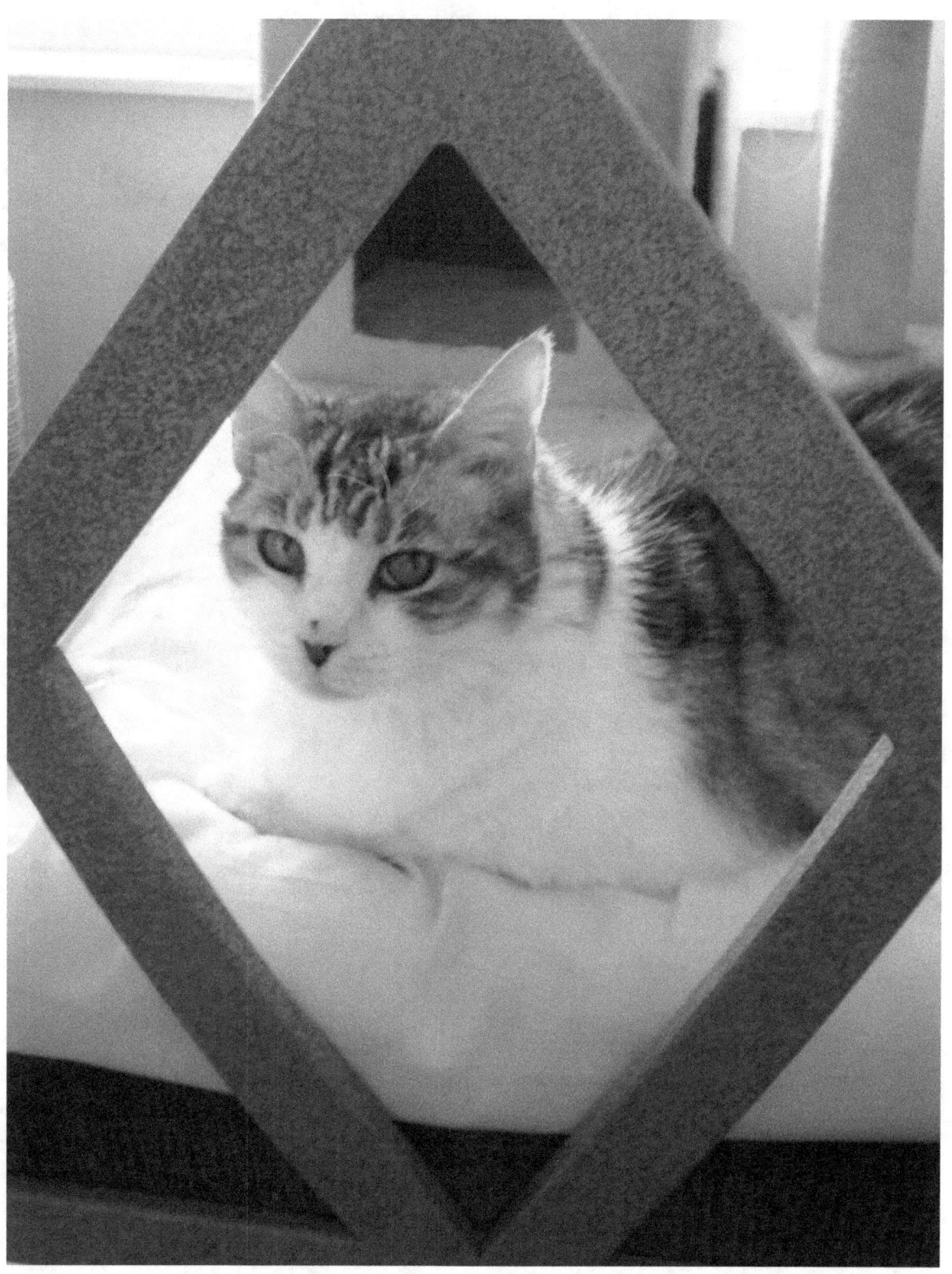

My mommy says no one loves me more than she does.

Guess what, mommy. I feel that way about you.

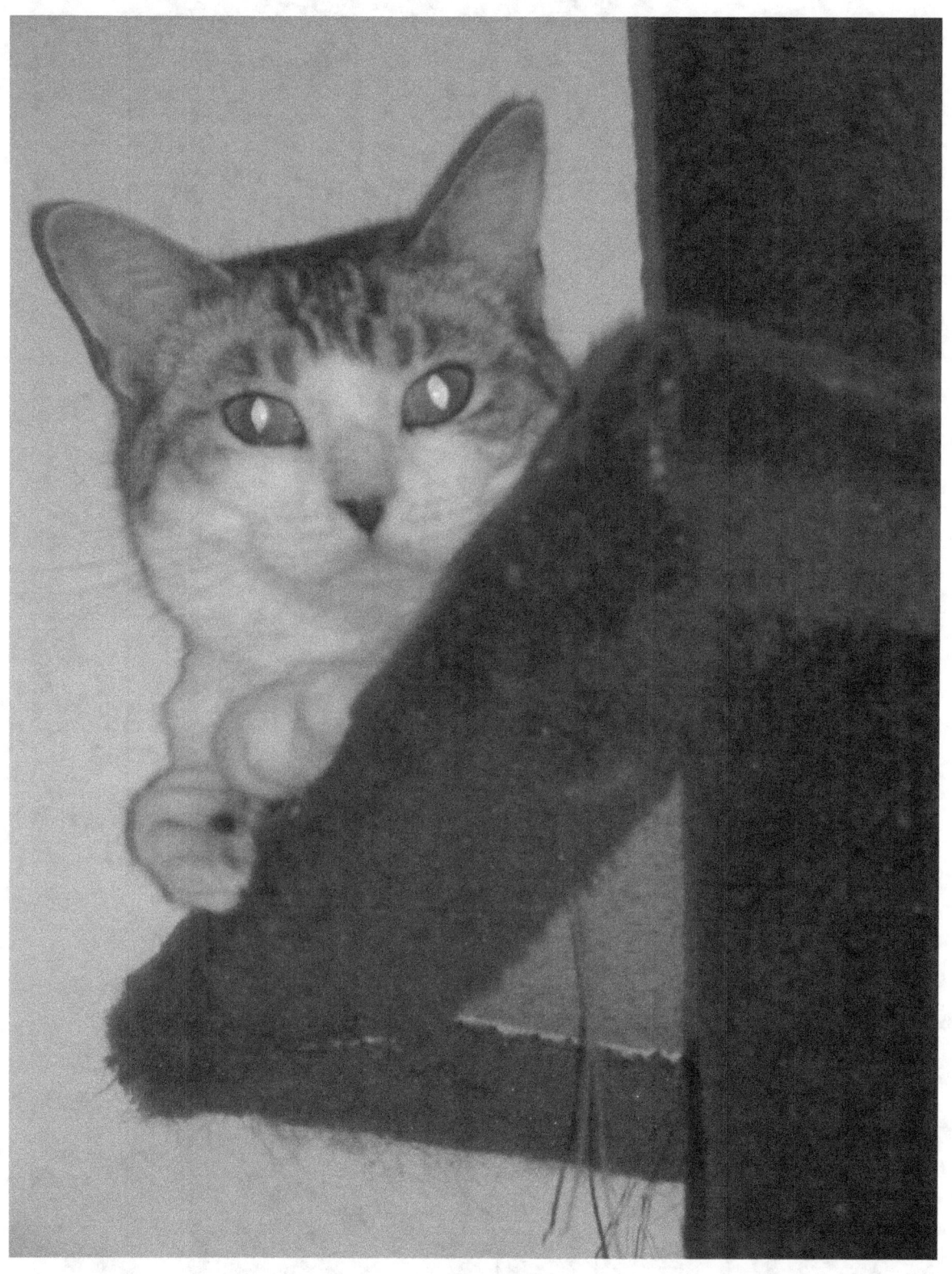

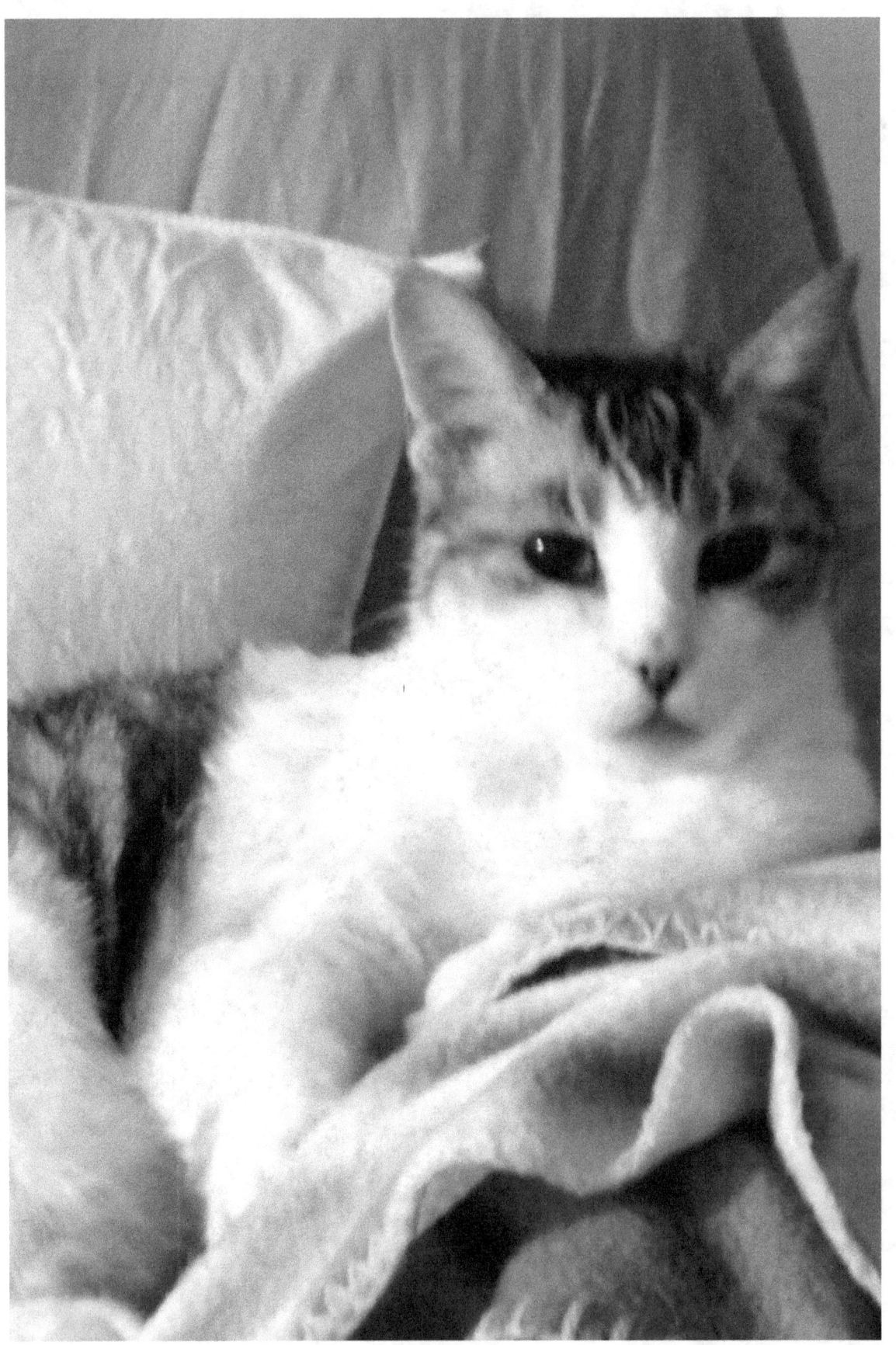

Moira

Adopted: May 2009

Died: June 9 2019

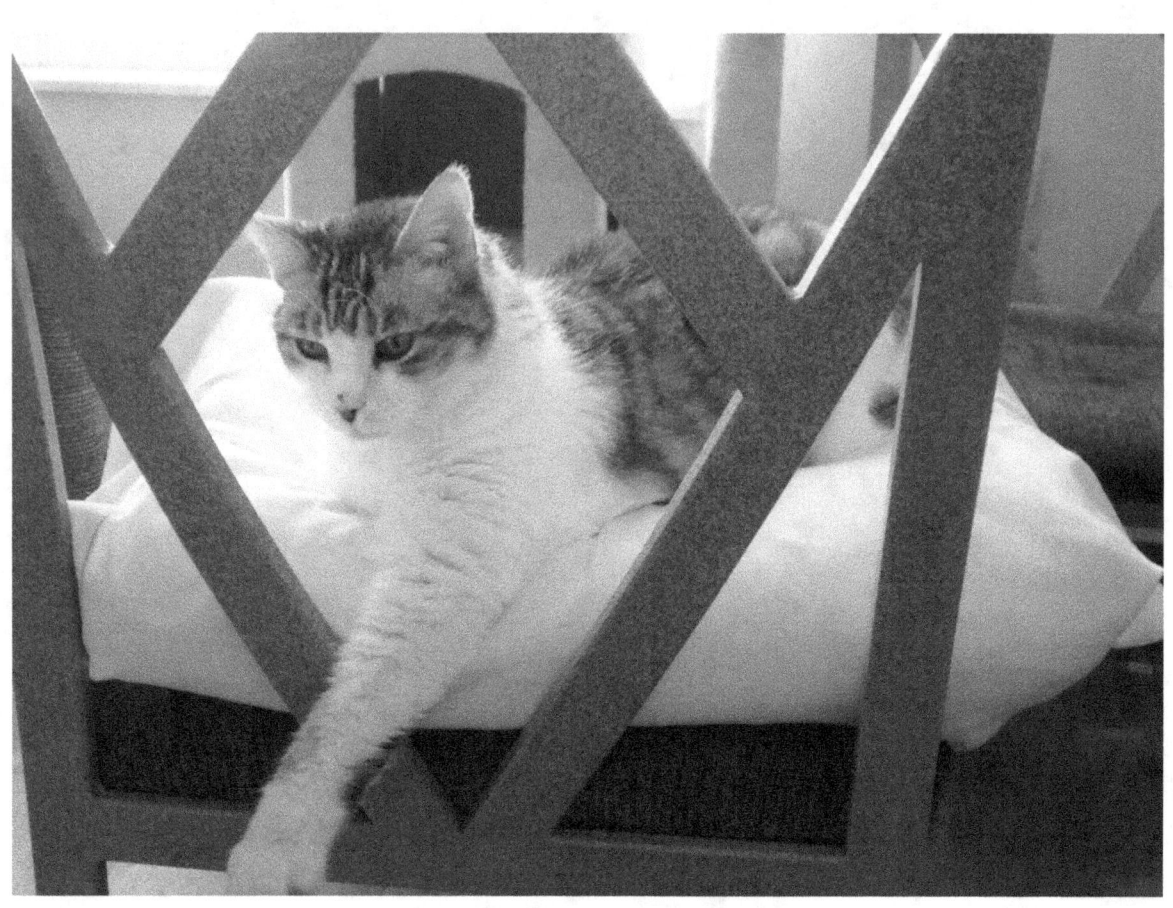

This book is in honor and memory of my 4 legged child, my best friend, and my companion. Moira will always be special to me. She brought so much love and laughter into my life.

Selena Millman

June 24, 2019

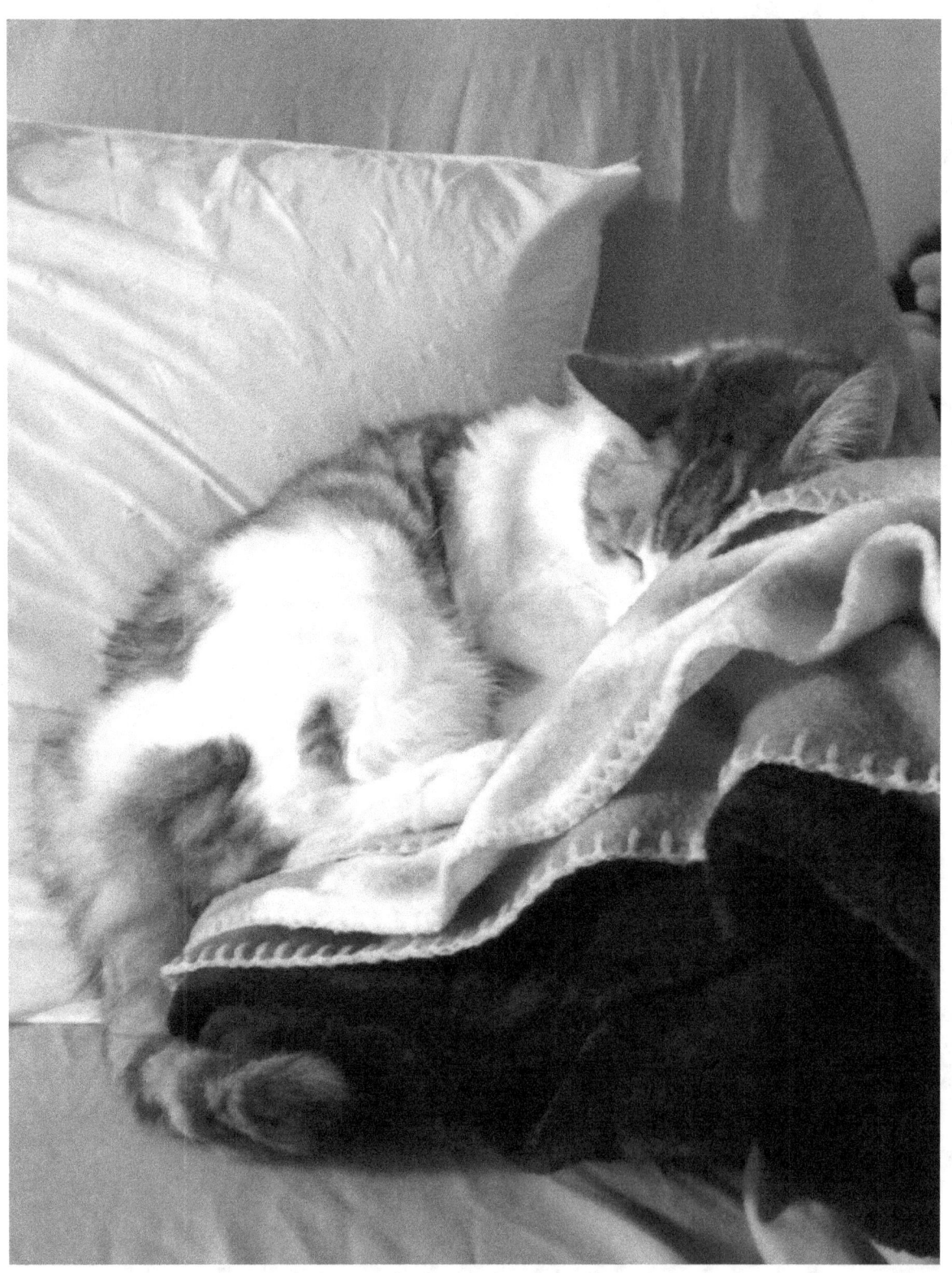

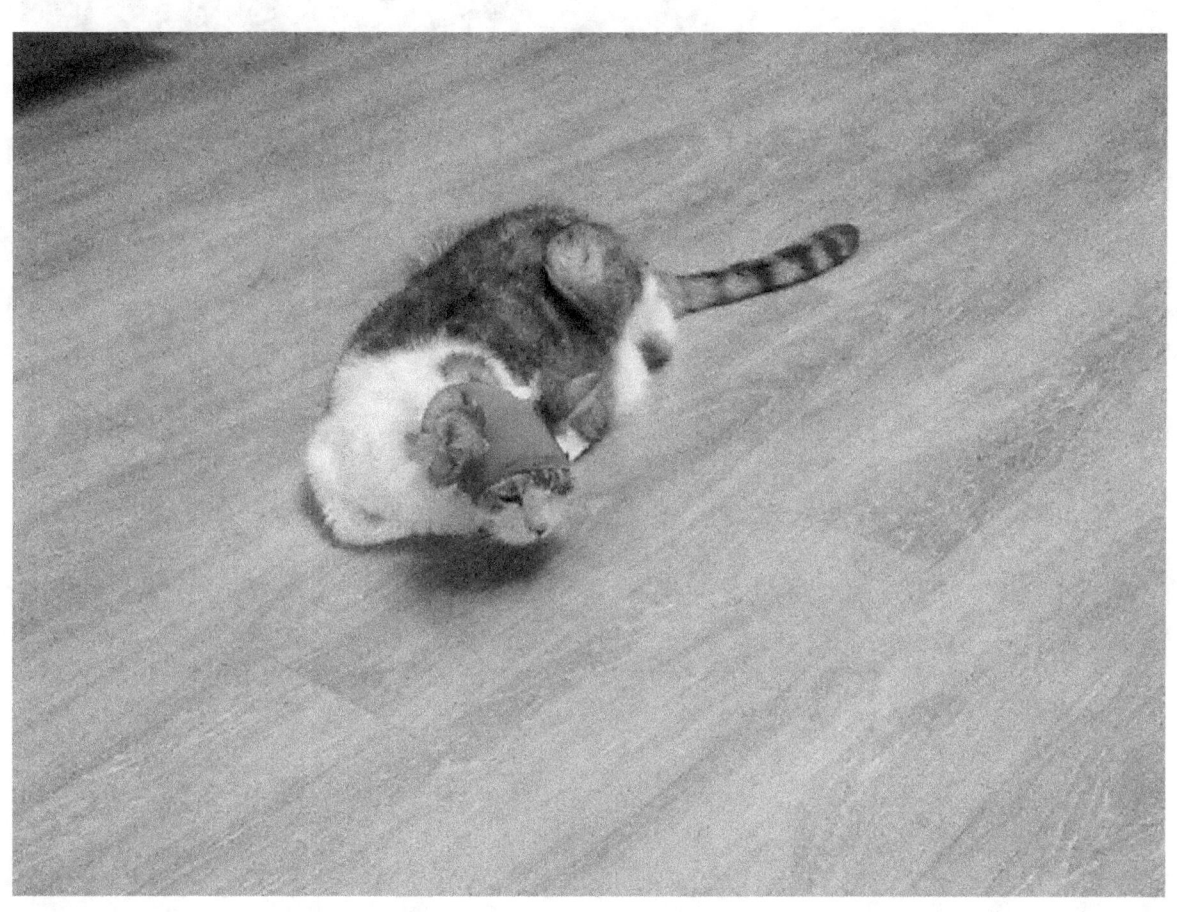

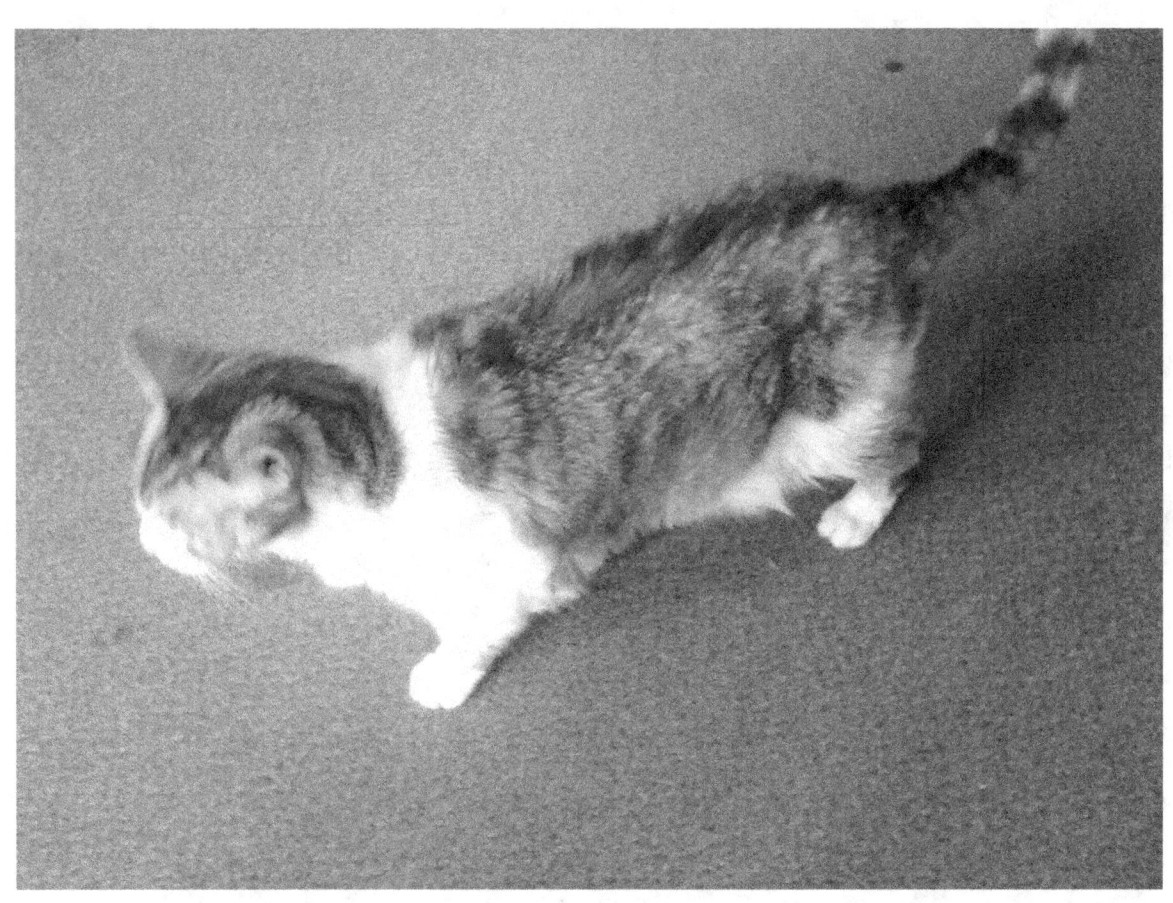

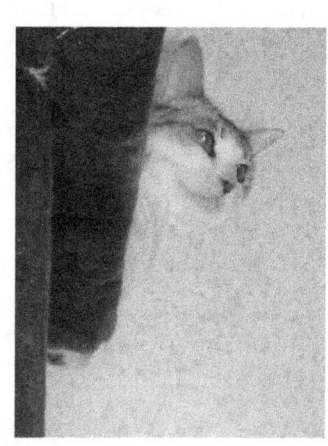

Moira Rules - The Photos

All color photos.

http://www.lulu.com/shop/selena-millman/moira-rules-the-photos/paperback/product-24150455.html

Moira Says
ISBN 9781300411819

Buy my Books and Photos at
http://www.lulu.com/heal4michael

Search Selena Millman at
http://www.amazon.com

Selena's Books & Devotions:
http://selenasbooksanddevotions.webs.com/

My Devotional Pages:
(Sermon Notes, Scripture, and Devotions)
http://heart4jesus.webs.com/
http://loveforjesus.webs.com/

My Books:
http://booksbyselena.webs.com/

Creative Page:
http://all4ty.webs.com/

www.ingramcontent.com/pod-product-compliance
Lightning Source LLC
Chambersburg PA
CBHW081313180526
45170CB00007B/2691